DIESEL MECHANIC MCQ

DIESEL MECHANIC MCQ

MANOJ DOLE

Digitization is the need of the time. In the future, training in industrial training institutes will need to be conducted using online internet to make training more convenient and easy. E-books containing a set of MCQ questions will be made available to the trainees as they need to be more accustomed to the multiple choice questions MCQ to prepare for the online exams taking place in their industrial training institutes.

With all these factors in mind, Mr. Manoj Madhukar Dole Instructor, Industrial Training Institute, Satara, has written books according to the new annual system and NSQF-5 syllabus. And they've created theoretical mobile apps and blogs to make training easier, and made all these educational materials available for download on the world famous websites Google Play Store, Amazon and Apple Book Store.

The books were published by Hon'ble Joint Director Shri Rajendra Ghume Saheb Regional Office of Vocational Education and Training, Pune on 9/1/2019, at this time Shri Prakash Saigavkar Saheb Principal Government Industrial Training Institute Aundh Pune, Shri Tukaram Misal Saheb Principal Govt. Q. Sanstha Satara, Shri Sachin Dhumal Saheb District Vocational Education and Training Officer Satara, Shri Yatin Pargaonkar Saheb Principal Govt. Q. Sanstha Kolhapur, Shri Vikas Teke Saheb Inspector Vocational Education and Training Regional Office Pune, Palekar Foods Products Pvt. Ltd. Entrepreneurial Chairman of Satara Mr. Nilkanthrao Palekar Saheb, Chairman of Hira Foods Mr. Ibrahim Baba Tamboli Saheb, Mrs. Shalmali Pawar Headmaster Government Technical School Center Satara and other dignitaries were present on the occasion.

Contents

Prologue

Diesel Mechanic MCQ is a simple e-Book for ITI Engineering Course Mechanic Diesel, Sem- 1 & 2, NSQ F-5 Syllabus in 2022 Syllabus in 2018,. It contains objective questions with underlined & bold correct answers MCQ covering all topics including all about the latest & Important about tools & equipment, raw materials, Measuring, Marking tools, basic fastening and fitting operations, welding joints by using Arc and gas welding, hydraulics and pneumatics components, Air and Hydraulic Brake system, Diesel Engine of LMV, Cylinder Head , valve train , Piston, connecting rod assembly crankshaft, flywheel and mounting flanges, spigot and bearings, camshaft, Cooling, lubrication, Intake & Exhaust system of Engine, Starter, alternator and lots more.

Foreword

Vocational education and training is imparted through the Department of Vocational Education and Training through the Department of Business Education and Business Practical to supply multi-skilled artisans in line with the rapidly growing demand in the industrial sector in the 21st century. All the occupations within the institutions are important, as the trainees from these occupations develop multi-skills as per the demands of the industry.

with the noble intention of making available MCQ e-books suitable for all businesses, considering that all the examinations in all the industries in the industrial sector are conducted online and include MCQ method questions. Mr. Manoj Madhukar Dole has written a very good e-book on MCQ method as per the new annual syllabus. This e-book will definitely be a guide for all the trainees, trainee candidates, training instructors and others concerned.

The author of the book is Mr. Manoj Madhukar Dole, Instructor Gov. ITI Satara has 17 years of training experience. Written as a new annual pattern, this e-book incorporates modern digital QR Code technology to understand the layout, simple language, and simple syntax, diagrams and videos for each subject. So I am sure that this e-book will definitely be useful for in-depth study and exam practice. The work they have done is certainly commendable.

Mr. Tukaram Misal

Principal Government Industrial Training Institute Satara.

Preface

DGET New Delhi and CSTARI Kolkata have been implementing an annual pattern for all businesses in ITI since the August 2018 session. The examination system will also be changed and it will be online from this year and since all the questions are of Objective Type (MCQ), the trainees are in dire need of in-depth study. It is with this in mind that we are delighted to present the books based on the old NIMI pattern and a complete overview of the new annual pattern, and we hope that these books will be a guide for all business directors and trainees. Is.

For writing these books, Johar Awate Saheb, Principal of ITI Akluj. Former Principal of ITI Satara Saigavkar Saheb, Assistant Director Shri Chandrakant Dhekne Saheb Regional Office of Vocational Education and Training, Pune, District Vocational Education and Training Officer Sachin Dhumal Saheb and Headmaster Government Technical School Kendra Shalmali Pawar Madam and son Adhiraj Dole, mother Kusum Dole, I am very grateful to my father Madhukar Dole and wife Ashwini Dole for their special guidance and cooperation from time to time.

Also, in a very short period of time, the book was reviewed by Shri Rajendra Ghume Saheb, Joint Director, Vocational Education and Training Regional Office, Pune, for his invaluable time in publishing the book. I am sincerely grateful for their feedback.

I am grateful to the Instructor of ITI Satara for there continuous support from the very beginning of writing the book.

From this book, I consider myself blessed to have shared my thoughts on e-learning with you. I will not claim that this book is perfect, because considering the perfection, this book is an attempt and is in its infancy. They will be valuable for improvement if they are tested and suggested.

Manoj Dole
Dated 9/1/2019

Acknowledgements

The industrial training and theoretical examination system of our industrial training institutes and these changes have been accepted by the craft instructors and the trainees. Theoretical examinations conducted in your industrial training institutes are also conducted online. Since these examinations are of multiple choice MCQ method, the trainees will need to get more practice of such questions.

With all these considerations in mind, Mr. Manoj Madhukar, Director, Dole Crafts, Katari Industrial Training Institute, Satara, has done a thorough study and with his diligent work and added his keen intellect, according to the new annual system and NSQF-5 syllabus, e-book of Katari and other machine trades. -Book) and they have created mobile apps and blogs on theoretical topics to make training easier and have made all these educational materials available for download on the world famous websites Google Play Store, Amazon and Apple Book Store. Training has been made easier by creating a print version and using advanced techniques like QR Code.

All these educational materials will definitely be a guide for all the trainees for in-depth study and for the craft instructors and other concerned who are imparting vocational training.

CHAPTER ONE

Diesel Mechanic MCQ Drawing

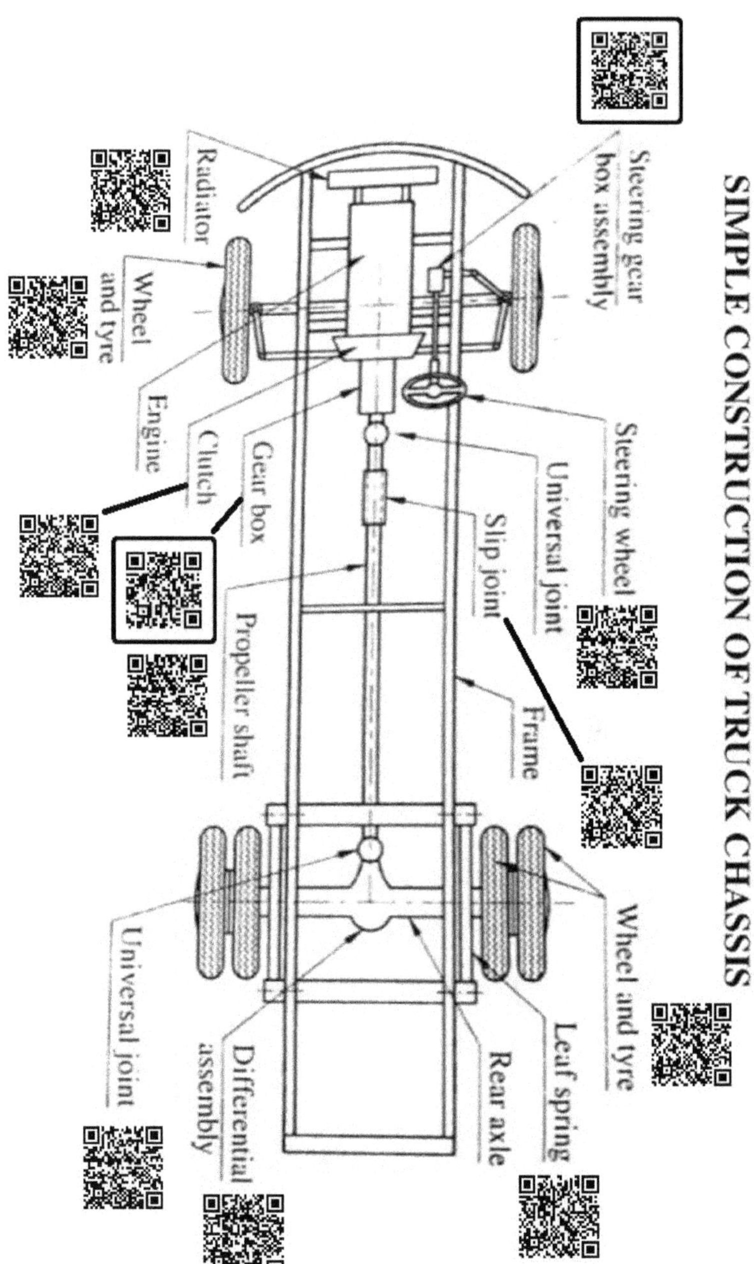

Truck Chassis

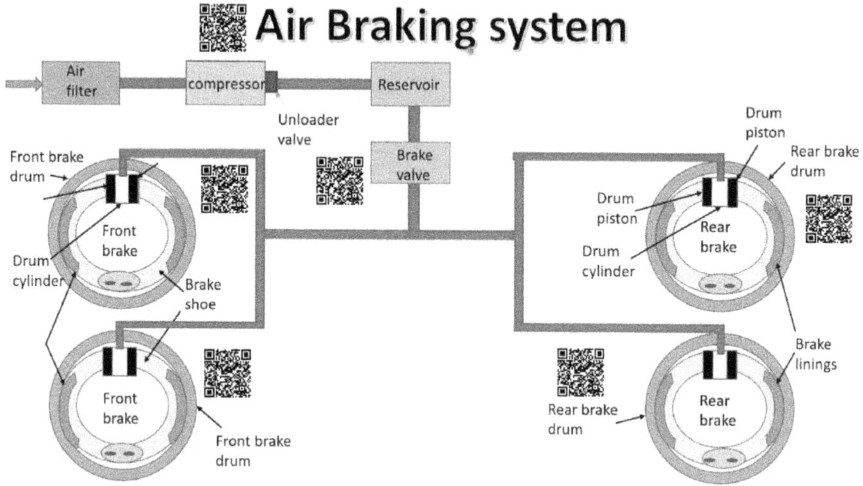

Air Brake System

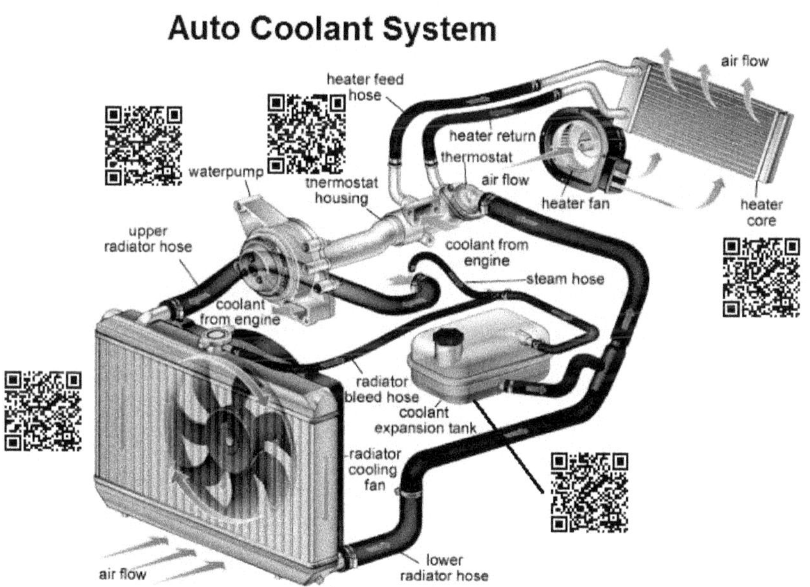

Coolant System

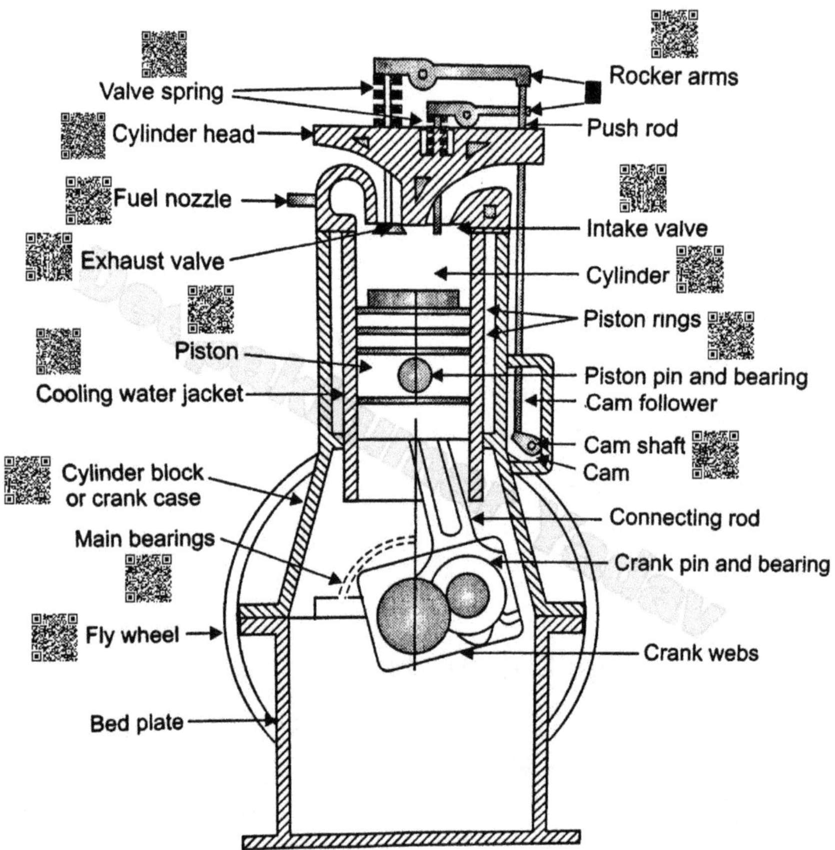

Components of Diesel Engine

Diesel Engine

Car Fuel System
EGR
valve
air injection
check valve
purge
valve
muffler
tail pipe
exhaust manifold
fuel tank
air pump
fuel
delivery line
oxygen
sensor
fuel vapor
vent line
resonator
fuel injector
intake manifold
oxygen
sensor
catalytic
converter
fuel tank
pressure sensor

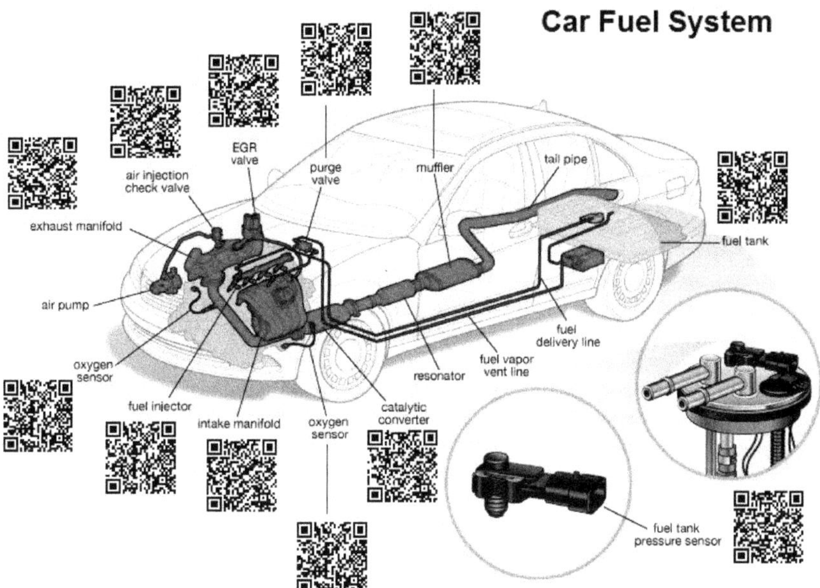

Fuel System

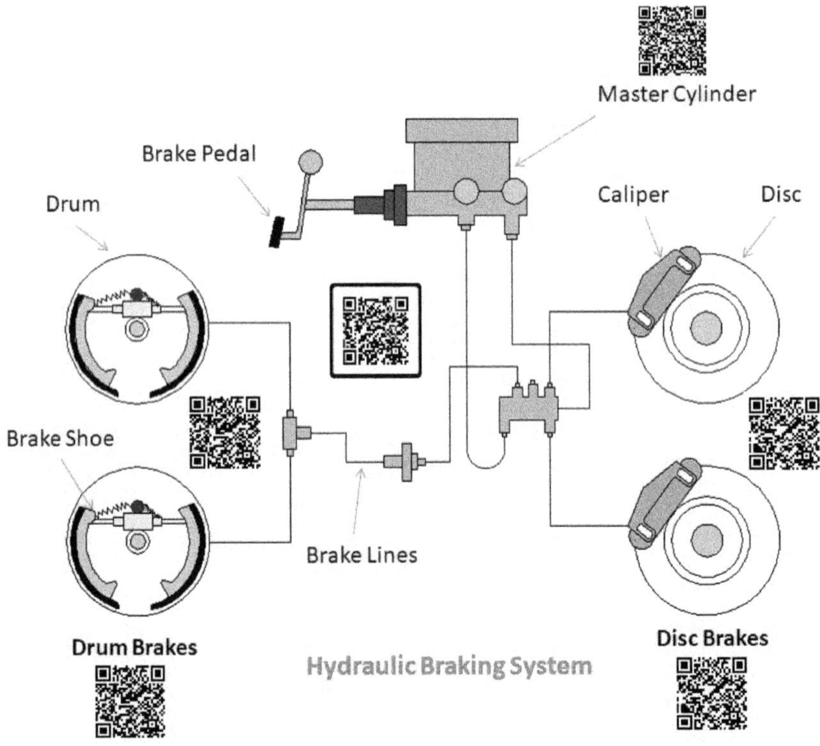

Hydraulic-Braking-System

Multi Point Fuel Injection Syastem

D- MPFI & L- MPFI

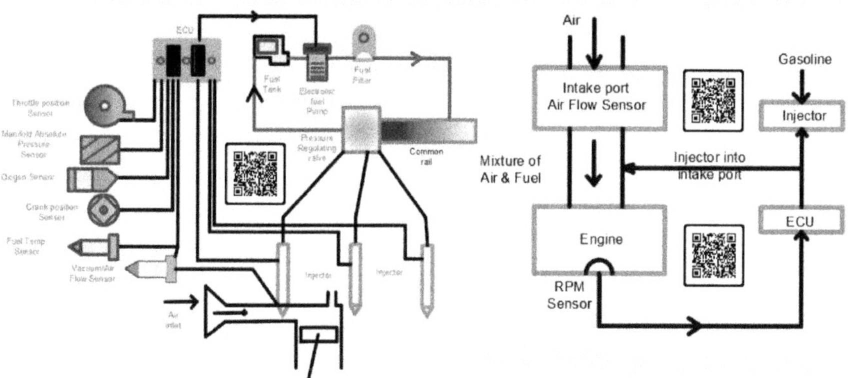

MPFI System

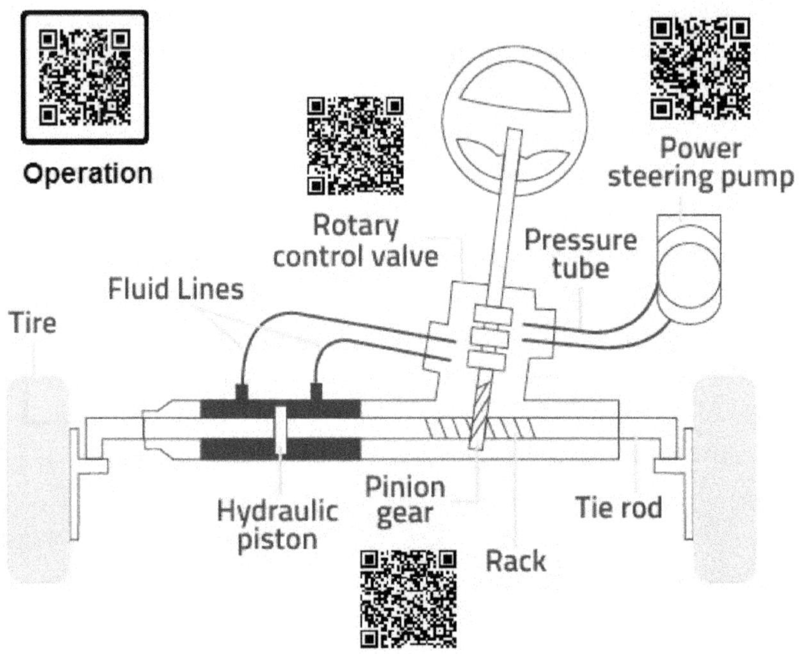

Power Steering System

Power Steering System

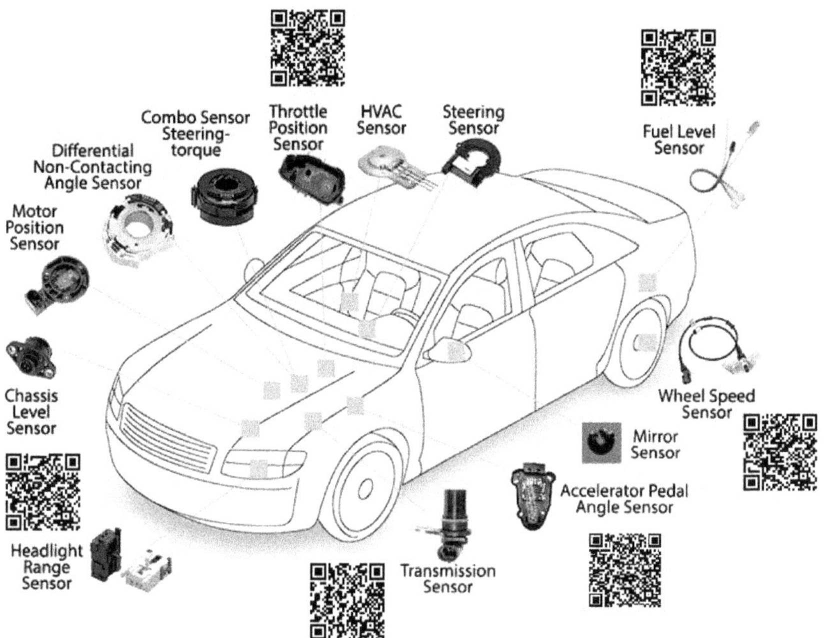

Car Sensor System

Sensor Systems

CHAPTER TWO

Diesel Mechanic MCQ

01] In case of bleeding, take treatment Of

D] Cold 3" and rest

<u>A] Spray cold water</u>

B] Bandage immediately -----.

B] Enquire about the accident thought treatment

02] In case of an accident, the victim should im

A] Asked to take rest

<u>C] Attended immediately</u>

D] leave him

03] First aid is given to an injured or ill person primarily....

A] Save life

B] Prevent further deterioration of the muff's

C] Give best possible comfort

<u>D] All of these</u>

04] Colour code for Bins for waste paper segregation is -----

<u>A] blue Colour</u>

B] Yellow Colour

C] Red Colour

D] Green Colour

05] In Japanese Seiko stands for --------------

<u>A] Shine</u>

B] Sort

C] Standardize

D] Sustain

06] Benefit of SS system is ------

A] Increase in productivity

B] Increase in quality

C] Reduction in wastage of time

D] All of these

07] Safety is -----------

A] Nobody's business

B] Every bodise business

C] Some bodies business

D] The organization business

08] For basic categories of safety signs are available The meaning of "prohibition" sign ----

A] Shows it must not be done

B] Shows what must be done

C] Warns the hazard or danger

D] Gives information of safety provision

09] Which one is a workshop safety?

A] Keep shop floor clean and free from grease, oil or other slippery materials

B] Stop the machine before changing the speed

C] Don't use cracked or chipped tools

D] Don't try to stop a running machine with hand

10] In Personal Protect Equipment (PPE] HELMET is used to

A] Protect head

B] Protect eyes

C] Protect hands

D] Protect ears

11] Which of the following belongs to general safety?

A Have a worker in good attitude

B] The work clean and clear

C] Concentrate on your work

D] Keep the floor and gangways clean and clear

12] While grinding, which is used to protect the eyes?

A] Dark green glass

B] Mask

C] Sun glasses

D] Safety goggles

Grinding

13] Which of the following is done for machine safety?

A] Check the oil level before starting the machine

B] Do things in a methodical way

C] Keep the floor and gangways clean and clear

D] Don't use dies and scarves

14] ln Personal Protect Equipment (PPE], 'sleeves' is used to protect ----------

A] Face

B] Eyes

C] Ears

D] Hands

15] ABC stands for --------------

A] Automatic Breathing Control

B] Automatic Blood Control

C] Airway Breathing Circulation

D] Automatic Blood Circulation

16] To put off "Class B" fire, the type of fire extinguisher used is............

A] Dry power

B] Carbon dioxide

C] Jet of water

D] Foam type

fire extinguisher

17] Which type of fire extinguisher is used to put off general fire?

A] Water type Extinguisher

B] Foam type Extinguisher

C] Dry chemical powder Extinguisher

D] Carbon dioxide (C02] Extinguisher

18] One micrometer (U] is equal to...

A] 0.1mm

B] 0.01mm

C] 0.001mm

D] 0.0001mm

19] The calliper meant for measuring the width of a slot is...

A] Odd leg calliper

B] Outside calliper

C] Jenny calliper

D] Inside calliper

20] The size of the dividers are specified by the -----------

A] Total length of legs

B] Distance between the points when fully opened

C] Length of legs without points

D] Distance between the pivot and the point

21] The instrument used to mark parallel lines, parallel to the datum edge is -

A] Jenny caliper

B] Divider

C] Outside calliper

D] Inside calliper

Callipers

22] Which one of the following is an indirect measuring tool?

A] Outside caliper

B] Vernier calliper

C] Steel rule

D] Outside micrometer

23] The reference surface during marking is provided by the...

A] Surface gauge

B] Workpiece

C] Drawing of the work

D] Marking table surface

24] The part of the universal surface gauge which helps to draw a parallel line along a datum edge is the..

A] Rocker arm

B] Snug

C] Fine adjustment screw

D] Guide pins

25] Scribers are made of...

A] Mild steel

B] High carbon steel

C] Brass

D] Cast iron

Hammer

26] Portion of the hammer used for fixing the handle is...

A] Face

B] Peen

C] Cheek

D] Eye hole

27] Weight of the hammer for the marking purpose is...

A] 250g

B] 500g

C] 1 kg

D] 2 kgs
28] The size of the dividers are specified by the...
A] Total length of the legs
B] Distance between the points when fully opened
C] Length of legs without the points
D] Distance between the pivot and the point
29] Name the punch used to locate the centre.
A] Prick punch 30°
B] Prick punch 60°
C] Centre punch
D] Dot punch

centre punch

30] The point angle of centre punch is --------
A] 30°
B] 50°
c] 900
D] 1200
31] Punches are used for forming ---------of any shape
A] Holes
B] Mining
C] Knurling
D] Reaming
32] Generally the length of the handle of the vice is ----------
A] 1.5 times the normal size of the vice
B] 2.5 times the normal size of the vice
C] 3.5 times the normal size of the vice
D] 4.5 times the normal size of the vice
33] Bench vice spindle is made of ....
A] mild steel
B] Cast iron
C] Tool steel
D] Bronze

Bench vice

34] The vice clamps are used to...
A] Protect hard jaws
B] Clamp the work pieces rigidly
C] Protect the finished surfaces
D] Prevent the movable jaw being filed

35] The reference surface during marking is provided by the...
A] Surface gauge
B] Workpiece
C] Drawing of the work
D] Marking table surface
36] The size of an engineer's vice is specified by the...
A] Length of the movable jaw
B] Width of the jaws
C] Height of the vice
D] Maximum opening of the jaws
37] The point angle of scriber is -----------
A] 30°
B] 60°
C] 5° to 10°
D] 12° to 15°
38] The cutting angle for chipping cast iron is...
A] 37.5°
B] 55°
C] 60°
D] 90°
39] The chisel will dig into the material when...
A] The rake angle is more
B] The clearance angle is too low
C] The angle of inclination is more
D] The angle of inclination is too low
40] A slight convexity is given to the cutting edge to...
A] Cut curved surfaces
B] Cut sharp corners
C] Prevent digging of the ends
D] Allow the lubricant to enter
41] Surface plates are made of...
A] High grade cast steel
B] Fine-grained cast iron
C] Alloy steels
D] Wrought iron
42] Surface plates are specified by their length and breadth & are in
A] decimetre
B] Cubic meter

C] Cylindrical

43] Used on finished tubular wrench surfaces to avoid marking.

A] Stillson pipe

B] Chain wrench

C] Strap wrench

D] Footprint wrench

44] Used for gripping and turning pipes and round stocks in confined places.

A] Stillson pipe

B] Chain wrench

C] Strap wrench

D] Footprint wrench

45] Used for holding iarge diameter pipes.

A] Stillson pipe

B] Chain wrench

C] Strap wrench

D] Footprint wrench

46] Used for gripping and turning pipes,tubes and cylindricai rods.

A] Stillson pipe

B] Chain wrench

C] Strap wrench

47] Accommodates wheel hub bearings.

A] Kingpin

B] Spring pad

C] Stub axle shaft portion

D] Track rod ball joints

48] Pushes with drawal plate

A] Clutch cover

B] Release bearing

C] Release fingers

D] Clutch plate

49] **Takes thrust load**

A] Crankshaft

B] Flywheels

C] Torque wrench

D] Thrust bearing

50]Distributor shaft is supported by

A] ball bearing

B] shell bearing

C] bush bearing

D] needle bearing

51] in a metric micrometer, a complete revolution of thimble advances -----------

A] 0.01 mm

B] 0.25 mm

C] 0.50 mm

D] 1.00mm

Micrometer

52] Ratchet Stop in the micrometer helps to ------------

A] Control the pressure

B] lock the spindle

C] Adjust the zero error

D] Hold the work piece

53] 1000 micron means ------------

A] 1 mm

B] 1 m

C] 1000 mm

D] 10 cm

54] What is the zero reading of a 50-75 mm outside micrometer?

A] 0.000 mm

B] 0.01 mm

C] 25.00 mm

D] 50.00 mm

55] The value of the smallest division on sleeve of a metric outside micrometer is -----

A] 0.50 mm

B] 1.00 mm

C] 1.50 mm

D] 2.00 mm

56] Ratchet stop in the micrometer helps to ---------

A] control the pressure

B] Lock the spindle

C] Adjust the zero error

D] Hold the work piece

57] Least count of depth micrometer is

A] 0.5 mm

B] 0.2 mm

C] 0.001 mm

D] 0.01 mm

Depth micrometer

58] The least count of vernier calliper is (main scale = 49 division, vernier scale = 50 division]

A] 0.1 mm

B] 0.01 mm

C] 0.001 mm

D] 0.02 mm

59] The type of measurement made by using a Vernier Calliper is -------

A] Direct measurement

B] Indirect measurement

C] 90“] (a] 81 (b]

D] None of these

60] Telescopic gauges are used to measure holes and slots.

A] from 10 mm to 100 mm

B] from 12 mm to 152 mm

C] from 12.7 mm to 152.4 mm

D] none of the above.

Telescopic gauge

61] Small hole gauges are used to measure holes and slots.

A] below 10 mm

B] below 12.7 mm

C] below 20 mm

D] below 20.7 mm.

Dial test indicator

62] The dial test indicator shows the measurement as...

A] The actual size of the component

B] The difference between the two steps of 5 mm

C] The magnified small variations in sizes through a pointer

D] The direct reading of the dimension

63] Which one of the following is not correct about dial test indicator?

A] It has 100 divisions on its dial

B] Motion of the stem is transferred to the dial through Gear train.

C] Its accuracy is 0.1 mm

64] the feeler gauge is used for...

A] Checking surface roughness

B] Checking the radius of work pieces
C] Checking the gap between mating parts
D] Checking the accuracy of the hole locators

Feeler gauge

65] Threading tools are checked for accuracy for the 60° angle by using a
A] Thread plug gauge
B] centre gauge
C] screw pitch gauge
D] tool angle gauge

Centre gauge

66] The number of threads per inch can be checked with a
A] tool gauge
B] metric rule by counting
C] ring gauge
D] screw pitch gauge

screw pitch gauge

67] Used in air compressor
A] Pressure gauge
B] Oil tank
C] Oil spray gun
D] Car hoist
68] Used where bolt and threads are to be protected from damage.
A] Donald cap nut
B] Thumb nut
C] Hexagonal nut
D] Wing-nut
69] Used where frequent removal and fixing is required.
A] Donald cap nut
B] Thumb nut
C] Hexagonal nut
D] Wing-nut
70] Used in machine building and structure work.
A] Donald cap nut
B] Thumb nut
C] Hexagonal nut
D] Wing-nut
71] Used where frequent adjustments are to be made.
A] Donald cap nut

B] Thumb nut

C] Hexagonal nut

D] Wing-nut

72] Nylon inserts in the nut prevent loosening.

A] Locking plate

B] Wire lock

C] Self-locking nut

D] Sawn nut

73] A slot is cut halfway across the nut.

A] Locking plate

B] Wire lock

C] Self-locking nut

D] Sawn nut

74] Prevents slackening of two bolts.

A] Locking plate

B] Wire lock

C] Self-locking nut

D] Sawn nut

75] Prevents rotation of the top nut.

A] Lock-nut

B] Grooved nut

C] Self-locking nut

D] Sawn nut

76] Prevents loosening of nut by the use of a plate shaped to fit the nut.

A] Locking plate

B] Wire lock

C] Self-locking nut

D] Sawn nut

77] Hexagonal nut with the lower part made cylindrical and the recessed groove.

A] Lock-nut

B] Grooved nut

C] Self-locking nut

D] Sawn nut

78] Reduces the height of rivet head above the meta\ surface

A] Countersunk head

B] Flat head

C] Pan head

D] Mushroom
79] commonly used for structural work.
A] Countersunk head
B] Flat head
C] Pan head
D] Snap head
80] Ammonium chloride is used as a flux for soldering...
A] steel
B] aluminium
C] galvanized iron
D] stainless steel
81] Soldering of M.S sheets takes place at a temperature of...
A] 150◦C
B] 250◦C
C] 400◦C
D] 850◦C
82] In soldering operation the base metal is...
A] not heated
B] heated to 200◦C
C] heated to 650◦C
D] heated to red hot condition
83] Rivets for Joining sheets to thick plates.
A] Countersunk head
B] Flat head
C] Pan head
D] Mushroom
84] Rivets for Joining sheet metal.
A] Countersunk head
B] Flat head
C] Pan head
D] Mushroom
85] Rivets for Heavy fabrication work.
A] Countersunk head
B] Flat head
C] Pan head
D] Mushroom
86] Soft soldering is done

A] below 450◦ C

B] above 450◦C

C] at 900◦C

D] above 1000◦C

87] Brazing is done

A] at 1900◦C

B] above 450◦C

C] at 1000◦C

D] below 450◦C

88] A brazed joint is

A] weaker than a soldered joint

B] stronger than a solder join

C] stronger than a welded joint

D] weaker than a silver soldered joint

89] A hole is drilled between crankshaft main journal and crank pin for

A] balancing of crankshaft

B] reducing crankshaft weight

C] lubricating connecting rod bearings

D] reducing crankshaft vibrations

90]In a dry sump lubrication system, a scavenging pump is used to

A] pump oil from sump to tank

B] pump oil directly to all moving parts

C] develop additional oil pressure

D] pump oil from tank to sum

91] Excessive oil pressure in the lubrication system may be due to

A] less quantity of engine oil in sump

B] incorrect adjustment of relief valve

C] less suction effect on the suction pipe

D] none of the above

92] when oil pressure increases above set limit, oil returns to sump through

A] pressure relief valve

B] by pass valve

C] oil filter

D] oil pump

93] For cutting thin tubing, the most suitable pitch of the hacksaw blade is...

A] 1.8mm

B] 1.4mm

C] 1mm

D] <u>0.8mm</u>

94] For cutting solid brass, the most suitable pitch of the hacksaw blade is...

A] <u>1.8mm</u>

B] 1.4mm

C] 1mm

D] 0.8mm

Hacksaw frame

95] A new hacksaw blade after a few strokes becomes loose because of the...

A] <u>Stretching of the blade</u>

B] Wing-nut threads being worn out

C] Wrong pitch of the blade

D] Improper selection of the set of saws.

96] While cutting small diameter pipes, it is advisable to watch regularly and ensure that...

A] The cut is along the curved line

B] <u>More saw teeth are in contract</u>

C] The work is not overheated

D] Proper balancing of hacksaw is maintained

97] The convexity of files helps...

A] To file concave surfaces

B] To file convex surfaces

C] <u>To prevent rounding of edges of work</u>

D. The file to become straight when pressure is applied

Files

98] Which file used for filling wood, leather and other soft material? .

A] Single cut file

B] Double cut file

<u>c] Rasp cut file</u>

D] Curved cut file

99] File used is used for ------------

A] Cleaning the work piece

C] Renewing the file teeth

<u>B] cleaning the file teeth</u>

D] Cleaning the chips

100] File card is used to --------

A] Clean the work piece

C] Renew the file teeth

B] Clean the file teeth

101] While grinding, which is used to protect the eyes?

A] Dark green glass

B] Mask

C] Sun glasses

D] Safety goggles

102] Grinding wheels made out of---------------- abrasive are most common because of its free and cool cutting action.

A] Aluminium oxide

B] Silicon oxide

C] Ammonium oxide

D] Carbide.

103] Which among the following abrasive is mostly used for cutting off wheels for cutting non metallic materials?

A] Aluminium oxide

B] Silicon carbide

C] Diamond

D] None of above

104] Which abrasive particle is used for grinding tungsten carbide tool insert?

A] Silicon carbide

B] A|203

C] Diamond

D] Corundum

105] Which of the following is the natural abrasive?

A] Aluminium oxide

B] Silicon

C] Boron carbide

D] Corundum

106] Which of the following is the manufactured abrasive?

A] Corundum.

B] Quartz

C] Silicon

D] Emery

107] Which abrasive particle is used for grinding steel fittings?

A] Silicon carbide

B] Aluminium oxide

C] Diamond.

D] boron oxide

108] What kind of abrasive cut of wheel should be used to cut concrete stone and masonry?

A] Silicon

B] Al203

C] Diamond grit

D] Glass

109] Which one of the following is important factor required to achieve the interchange ability in mass production? .

A] Geometrical accuracy.

B] Standardization

C] Dimensional accuracy

D] Surface finish

110] Interchange ability is normally applied for? _

A] Repairing of parts

B] Mass production

C] Single piece production

D] All of these

111] When tolerance given in one side of the basic dimension, it is called --------

A].Tolerance system

B] Unilateral tolerance

C] Bilateral tolerance

D] Allowance System

112] The measured Size Of the dimensions of a component as called---------

A] Basic size

B] Nominal Size

C] Allowed size

D] Actual size

113] In the drawing the dimensions of a shaft is shown 40i 0068/0042, which is the size of Shaft within the tolerance?

A] 4.0.64 mm

B] 40.042 mm

C] 40.000 mm

D] 39.998 mm

114] In Hole basic system ----------

A] The size of the shaft is made constant

B] The Size of the hole is made constant

C] Only 'allowance is given on the hole

D] The permissible tolerance are given on the hole and the Shaft

115] The Size of a component is given as 24 -0.1. What does -O.1 indicates? _

A] Upper deviation is + 0.1 mm .

B] Lower deviation is 0.0 mm

C] Fundamental deviation is 0.0 mm

D] Lower deviation is _0.1 mm

116] The tolerance of a hole iS the difference between the -------

A] Maximum hole Size and maximum Shaft size

B] Maximum hole size and maximum hole Size

C] Minimum'hole size and maximum Shaft Size

D] Minimum hole Size and minimum shaft Size

117] A hole whose lower deviation is zero is called basic hole. Which one of the following letter indicates basic hole?

A] E

B] F

C] G '

D] H

118] Which one having upper deviation zero?

A] Bassc Shaft

B] Basic hole

C] Tolerance

D] Clearance

119] A ball bearing on a shaft is type of fit? ,

A] Clearance fit

B] Driving fit

C] Shrinkage fit

D] None of the above

120] In the BIS system of limits and fits, the grade of tolerance are represented by number Symbols and there are ---------i

A] 14 grades of tolerance

B] 16 grades of tolerance

C] 18 grades of tolerance '

D] 20 grades of tolerance

121] A Product is said to have the quality when ....

A] Its shape and dimensions are within the limit

B] It is fit for use

C] It appears to be very good

D] The choice of material is right

122] The maximum clearance required between hole'30 +0.021, 0.000 and shaft 30 -0.110, 0.143 is.

A] 0.110 mm '

B]0.131 mm

C] 0.164 mm

D] 0.143 mm

123] A dimension is stated as 25 .1002 mm in a drawing. What is the tolerance?

A] +0.02 mm'

B] +0.04 mm

C] -0.02 mm

D] 25.00 mm

124] A pin is fitted in a hole. The tolerance zone of the pin is entirely above that of hole. The fit obtained will be?

A] Clearance fit

B] Transition fit

C] Interference fit

D] Running fit

125] Tolerance is given to the part size to............

A] Production the part within the required permissible size error

B] Increase the production

C] Decrease the Production

D] Finish the components approximately

126] Which one of the following is the clearance fit under the whole basic system?

A] 20 H7/p6'

B] 2067/211

C] ZOG/gll .

D] 20H/g11.

127] The three classes of fits as per BIS system aré ....

A] Clearance fit, interference fit and transition fit

B] Medium fit, push fit and tight fit

C] Flat fit, round fit and square fit

D] 'Sliding fit ', loose fit and shrinkage fit

128] Which one of the following tolerance specifications has a maximum dimensionless than 20 mm?

A] 20 +0.2,-0.3

B] 20 320.2

C] 20 -0.2, 0.3 e

D]m 20 +500, ~03

129] Difference between the maximum and minimum limit is --------------------

A] Single informant

B] Basic shaft

C] Clearance

D] Tolerance

130] A shaft 55 running freely in bush bearing the type of fit is ---------

A] Clearance fit

B] Driving plate

C] shrinkage fit

D] None of the above

131] The taper shank drills are held on the machine by means of...

A] Chucks

B] Sleeves

C] Drift

D] Vice

132] Drill chucks are fitted on the drilling machine spindle by means of a...

A] Knurled ring

B] Arbor

C] Drift

D] Pinion and key

Drilling

133] The Morse taper provided on drills ranges between...

A] MT 1 to MT 5

B] MT 1 to MT 4

C] MT 0 to MT 5

D] MT 0 to MT 4

134] A drift is used for...

A] Drawing a drill location

B] Fixing chuck on the machine spindle

C] Removing a broken drill from the work

D] Removing the drill from the machine spindle

135] When the taper shank of the drill is larger than the machine spindle, the device to hold the drill is a...

A] Drill sleeve

B] Taper socket

C] Drill drift

D] Chuck and key

136] The suitable cutting fluid for drilling mild steel in a drilling machine is...

A] Synthetic soluble oil

B] Neat oil

C] Distilled water

D] Soluble oil

137] A special feature of the radial drilling machine is...

A] It can be used for drilling with a H.S.S. drill

B] Table can be moved and set at any position

C] A variety of speeds is available

D] The spindle can be brought to any position

138] The point angle of drills depends on...

A] The size of the drill

B] The type of machine

C] The material of the work

D] The RPM of the drill

139] The point angle for a standard drill is...

A] 60◦

B] 108◦

C] 118◦

D] 135◦

140] The helical angle determines the...

A] Cutting angle

B] Chew angle

C] Rake angle

D] Lip angle

141] The clearance angle of the drill is between...

A] 3° to 5°

B] 8° to 12°

C] 12° to 20°

D] 15° to 20°

142] Drill chuck are held on the machine spindle by means of ------

A] arbor

B] Drift

C] draw-in bar

D] Chuck nut

143] Different speeds are obtained in a sensitive bench drilling machine by ----

A] Belt pulley mechanism

B] Hydraulic mechanism

C] Rack and Pinion mechanism

D] Cam and follower mechanism

144] Which one of the following is used only for finishing and maintaining correct form of thread?

A] Tap

B] Threading tool

C] Threading chaser

D] Tipped tool

Tap Die

145] A die in which more than one cutting operation is per formed in one stroke

A] Piercing die

B] Progressive die

C] Combination die

D] Compound die

146] A die in which cutting and non cutting operations are carried out per stroke.

A] Piercing die

B] Progressive die

C] Combination die

D] Compound die

147] A die in which two or more sequential operations are performed at two or more stations upon the work.

A] Piercing die

B] Progressive die

C] Combination die

D] Compound die

148] A die in which the shape of the punch and die are directly reproduced in the metal with little or no metal flow.

A] Progressive die

B] Combination die

C] Compound die

D] Forming die

149] The die used for producing any shape of holes.

A] Piercing die

B] Progressive die

C] Combination die

D] Compound die

150] The external threads on G.l.pipes are out easily

A] by tap sets

B] dies and die stocks

C] centre lathes

D] thread rollers.

Thread

151] A short reamer with an axial hole used with an arbor or mandrel is called -------

A] Parallel reamer

B] Adjustable reamer

C] Expansion reamer

D] Chucking reamer

152] Which one of the following machine reamers is used to correct the misalignment between the reamer axis and the work axis?

A] Floating blade reamer

B] Machine jig reamer.

C] Shell reamer

D] Chucking reamer

153] Tap are re sharpened by grinding -----

A] Hutes

B] Threads

C] Diameter

D] Relief

154] ln case of ant burr on slip gauge, it should be removed by

A] Filling

B] Lapping
C] Scraping
D] Grinding
155] The purpose for which lapping operation are carried out ---
A] To refine surface finish.
B] To improve quality of fit
C] To improve geometrical accuracy,
D] All the above
156] Lapping compound material is ----------
A] Sand stone
B] Diamond
C] Quartz
D] Corundum
157] When does the work piece get charged with the abrasive and cut the lap?
A] The work piece is harder than the lap
B] The work piece is softer than the lap
C] The lap is softer than the work piece
D] The lap is coarser than the work piece
158] The grooves are provided on the lapping plate for-----------..
A] Preventing distortion of the plate
B] Retaining lapping paste
C] Reducing friction
D] Collects the metal-chips
159] The following material is used for diamond lapping ....
A] H55
B] Copper '
C] Aluminium oxide,
D] High carbon steel
160] for making gutters, roof flashing, hoods etc.
A] Galvanised iron
B] Stainless steel
C] Copper sheet
D] Metal sheets
161] in dairies. food processing, kitchen ware etc.
A] Galvanised iron
B] Stainless steel
C] Copper sheet

D] Metal sheets

162] for making buckets, heating ducts, cabinets etc.

A] Galvanised iron

B] Stainless steel

C] Copper sheet

D] Metal sheets

163] in canneries and chemical plants Metal sheets

A] Galvanised iron

B] Stainless steel

C] Copper sheet

D] Metal sheets

164] Alloy steel, good corrosive resistance and welds easily

A] Black iron

B] Galvanised iron

C] Stainless steel

D] Aluminium

165] Cheapest, can be rolled to any desired thickness

A] Black iron

B] Galvanised iron

C] Stainless steel

D] Aluminium

166] Provides change of direction with a long radius at right angle.

A] Plug

B] Elbow

C] Bend

D] Reducer 'T' branczh

167] A branch type hand operated pipe bending machine is used to bend

A] P.V.C.pipes

B] onduit pipes

C] G.I.pipes

D] copper pipes.

168] The inner formers of a hydraulic pipe bending machine are able to bend pipes up to a diameter of

A] 40mm

B] 100mm

C] 20mm

D] 75mm

169] Provides deviation of 90°

A] Plug
B] Elbow
C] Bend
D] Reducer 'T' branczh
170] Used for closing a line which has an internal thread.
A] Plug
B] Elbow
C] Bend
D] Reducer 'T' branczh
171] Provides deviation of'45°
A] Bend
B] Reducer 'T' branczh
C] Elbow
D] Tee piece
172] Provides outlet at right angles to the run.
A] Bend
B] Reducer 'T' branczh
C] Elbow
D] Tee piece
173] Used where a change in ' pipe diameter is required.
A] Bend
B] Reducer 'T' branczh
C] Elbow
D] Tee piece
174] Selection of a former depends on the
A] outside diameter of the pipe
B] wall thickness of the pipe
C] bore diameter of the pipe
D] all the above.
175] The included angle of a pipe thread is
A] 60°
B] 47°
C] 55°
D] 45°
176] G.l.pipes are available in a standard length of
A] 5 metres
B] 18"
C] 6 metres

D] 16 feet.

177] The standard pipe fittings are provided with threads conforming with

A] BA

B] BSW

C] BSP

D] Metric.

178] The external threads on G.l.pipes are out easily

A] by tap sets

B] dies and die stocks

C] centre lathes

D] thread rollers.

179] Water flowing from tap even when firmly closed.

A] Spindle bent.

B] Defective washer.

C] Valve on the spindle loose.

D] Spindle thread worn-out.

180] Tap hard to turn on and off.

A] Spindle bent.

B] Defective washer.

C] Valve on the spindle loose.

D] Spindle thread worn-out.

181] Loud noise in the tap when turned on.

A] Spindle bent.

B] Defective washer.

C] Valve on the spindle loose.

D] Spindle thread worn-out.

182] G.l. pipes are provided externally with

A] no threads

B] parallel threads

C] tapered threads

D] neither parallel nor tapered threads.

183] in the pipe assembly, the hemp packing is used

A] for easy engagement

B] to fill the gap between threads

C] to avoid leakage

D] to get tight fitting.

184] The sealing compound shall be applied on the pipe threads

A] before hemp packing
B] after hemp packing
C] before and after temp packing
D] none of the above.
185] Ohms is unit for
A] Resistance
B] Voltmeter
C] Ammeter
D] Cell tester
186] Fitted on panel board
A] Resistance
B] Voltmeter
C] Ammeter
D] Cell tester
187] If the thin cables are used for starter motor
A] Cable wilt get heated up
B] Voltage drop
C] Supply lesser current
D] Supply more current.
188] The main feed wires from the battery consists the main colour of
A] White
B] Brown.
D] red
D] Black
189] Earth circuit colour
C] Blue/red
D] Red
E] Black
F] White
190] Front parking lamp colour
A] Brown
B] Yellow
C] Blue/red
D] Red
191] ignition circuit colour
C] Blue/red
D] Red
E] Black

F] White

192] Generating circuit colour

A] Brown

B] Yellow

C] Blue/red

D] Red

193] Head light circuit colour

A] Brown

B] Yellow

C] Blue/red

D] Red

194] Battery feed circuit colour

A] Brown

B] Yellow

C] Blue/red

D] Red

Lead acid battery in vehicle

195] Measures voltage of battery

A] Resistance

B] Voltmeter

C] Ammeter

D] Cell tester

196] A multimeter cannot measure...

A] current

B] potential difference

C] capacitance

197] The earth conductor provides a path to ground for..

A. leakage current

B] over current

C] high voltage

D] circuit current

198] Heat developed in a conductor is proportional to the...

A] square of the power

B] square of the resistance

C] square of the current

D] square of the time

200] Separates the points

A] Solenoid Switch

B] Actuating wire (when heated]
C] Ballast Resistors
D] Actuating wire (when cooled]
201] Limits the current to the points
A] Solenoid Switch
B] Actuating wire (when heated]
C] Ballast Resistors
D] Actuating wire (when cooled]
202] Closes the points
A] Solenoid Switch
B] Actuating wire (when heated]
C] Ballast Resistors
D] Actuating wire (when cooled]
203] Specific gravity of battery electrolyte is checked by
A] ammeter
B] Voltmeter
C] Hydrometer
204] Power companies are interested in improving the power factor to
A] reduce line current
B] increase motor efficiency
C] increase volt-amperes
D] decrease power
205] Moving coil instrument works on the effect of...
A] chemical effect
B] heating effect
C] electrostatic effect
D] electromagnetic effect
206] Produces magnetic field
A] Armature
B] Spark plug
C] Condenser
D] Horse shoe
207] Rotates between magnetic poles
A] Armature
B] Spark plug
C] Condenser
D] Horse shoe
208] The ends of stator winding attached to the

A] Field coil
B] Carbon brush
C] Copper brush
D] Diodes.
209] Absorbs the heat in diodes
A] Diode
B] Stator
C] Fingers
D] Heat sink
210] Made of silicon
A] Diode
B] Stator
C] Fingers
D] Heat sink
211] The pressure of acetylene gas for gas cutting a 10mm M.S plate is...
A] 0.15 kgf/cm2
B] 0.5 kgf/cm2
C] 1.0 kgf/cm2
D] 1.5 kgf/cm2
212] What size of the cutting nozzle you will select for cutting 10mm thick mild steel?
A] 0.8 mm
B] 1.2 mm
C] 1.6 mm
D] 2.0 mm
213] The angle of filler rod in case of rightward welding technique is...
A] 10 to 20◦
B] 20 to 30◦
C] 30 to 40◦
D] 40 to 50◦
214] One of the advantages of the high pressure system of gas welding is...
A] it is cheaper
B] it is portable
C] it is less dangerous
D] it does not require a skilled welder
215] The function of a gas regulator is...
A] get different types of flames

B] mix the gases in the required proportion

C] change the volume of gas flowing to the blow pipe

D] set the working pressure

216] For welding a lap fillet joint in vertical position by gas what should be the angle of below pipe to the line of weld?

A] 30◦ to 40◦

B] 45◦to 50◦

C] 60◦ to 70◦

D] 75◦ to 80◦

217] Which metal pipe should NOT be used for passing acetylene gas in order to avoid explosions?

A] galvanized iron

B] stainless steel

C] mild steel

D] cooper

218] he percentage of carbon in acetylene gas is...

A] 99%

B] 92.3%

C] 89.1%

D] 85.3%

219] Acetylene gas contains

A] calcium, carbon and hydrogen

B] calcium and hydrogen

C] calcium, carbon, hydrogen and oxygen

D] carbon and hydrogen

220] In an acetylene purifier the sulphureted and phosphorated hydrogen are removed by...

A] pumice

B] water

C] filter wool

D] purifying chemicals

221] One of the functions of flux in gas welding is...

A] dissolve the metal oxides

B] reduce the melting point of mental

C] increase the flame temperature

D] increase the root penetration

222] On which of the following factors, the choice of flux for gas welding depend?

A] type of material to be joined

B] type of edge penetration

C] type of fuel gas

D] type of flame used

223] The divergence allowance required for gas welding a 300mm long copper butt joint is...

A] 1 to 2 mm

B] 2 to 3 mm

C] 3 to 4 mm

D] 4 to 5 mm

224] The type of edge preparation done for gas welding a 4mm thick copper butt joint is...

A] single bevel

B] single V

C] double V

D] square

225] The size of nozzle used to gas weld 3.15 mm thick aluminium butt joint is...

A] 13

B] 10

C] 7

D] 5

226] What is the value of preheating temperature for gas welding of aluminium?

A] 100 to 120°C

B] 150 to 180°C

C] 180 to 200°C

D] 210 to 250°C

227] Name the tool used to make and finish the leak proof joints of a pipe T joint

A] groover

B] setting hammer

C] creasing hammer

D] round bottom stake

228] The angle of vee groove of a single vee but joint for cast iron welding is...

A] 60°

B] 70◦

C] 80◦

D] 90◦

229] Shielded metal arc welding is classified under the process of...

A] electric resistance welding

B] special welding

C] electric arc welding

D] electro gas welding

230] How to specify the size of an electrode holder?

A] by its weight

B] by its shape

C] by its current carrying capacity

D] by the metal used for making it

231] The current set for a 3.15mm medium coated mild steel electrode is...

A] 50 to 80 amp

B] 90 to 120 amp

C] 120 to 150 amp

D] 150 to 170 amp

232] A long arc is used in...

A] welding with a low hydrogen electrode

B] horizontal position

C] plug or slot welding

D] cast iron welding

233] If the travel speed of electrode is high, which type of weld defect you will get on a T fillet joint?

A] overlap

B] slag inclusion

C] excessive reinforcement

D] lack of root penetration

234] Which weld defect occurs on a lap fillet joint due to improper weaving of the electrode in the covering/final run?

A] crack

B] undercut

C] lack of fusion

D] edge of plate melted off

235] Which one of the following is used in the oxy-arc cutting process?

A] flux coated solid electrode

B] bare wire tubular electrode

C] flux coated tubular electrode

D] bare tungsten arc cutting electrode

236] The electrode holder in a carbon arc cutting equipment is made up of...

A] plain carbon steel

B] galvanized iron

C] aluminium

D] copper

237] Main purpose Of annealing is -----------.

A] to improve machinability

B] to improve magnetism

C] to increase hardness

D] to increase toughness

238] The carbon percentage in H.S.S. tool is -------

A] 0.75 to 1.00 %

B] 1.00 to 2.00 00

C] 0.60 to 0.75 %

D] 0.02 to 0.03 %.

239] Which one of the following is the resistance of a metal to elastic deformation?

A] Ductility.

B] Strength

C] Stiffness

D] Toughness

240] The process of heating and cooling to change the structure of steel for obtaining the required properties is called

A] Hardening

B] Normalizing

C] Heat treatment

D] Tempering

241] The main purpose of annealing is to

A] Increase the hardness

B] Increase the toughness

C] Improve machinability

D] Improve distortion

242] The purpose of normalizing steel is to -----------

A] Remove the induced Stress

B] Improve genes and reduce brittleness

C] Soften the metal

D] Increase the surface?

243] Which one of the following process is used for hardenmg the outer 5" Annealing

A] Hardening

B] Tempering

<u>C] Case Hardening</u>

D] Tear surface

244] The purpose of producmg a component with tough and ductIle core and hard ou is known as......

A] Hardening

<u>B] Case hardening</u>

C] Tempering

D] annealing

245] Lower critical temperature of high carbon steel while hardening is ----------

A] 9600C

B] 900°C

<u>c] 7230 c</u>

D] 56O C

246] The process of Changing the structure and thus changing the properties by heating and 'cooling is known as --

<u>A] Heat treatment</u>

B] Alloying

C] Tempering

D] None of these

247] For refining the grain structure which one of the following heat treatment processes 'Is adopted.

A] Annealing

B] Hardening

C] Tempering

<u>D] Normalising</u>

248] Annealing is performed on iron and steel ---------

A] To remove internal stresses

B] To reduce hardness

C] To improve machinability

<u>D] All of these</u>

249] Which one of the following does not fall under the stages of heat treatment?

A] Heating

B] Cleaning

C] Quenching

D] Soaking

250] Fluid under pressures

A] To start heavy duty engine

B] Starter motor

C] Hydraulic cranking

D] Electric motor

251] Hydraulic floor jack is used

A] To remove king pin bush

B] To lift the wheel

C] To press the bush

D] Hold the job.

252] Which one of the following is the advantage of pneumatic system?

A] For low cost layout

B] For increasing the rate of production

C] For better working environment

D] All of these

253]The pressure of fluid in hydraulic brake system is governed by

A] boils law

B] Charles law

C] Pascal's law

D] none of the above laws

254] Allows fluid both way in and out of cylinder

A] Piston

B] Push Rod

C] Primary cup

D] Check valve

255] Seals the compensating port

A] Piston

B] Push Rod

C] Primary cup

D] Check valve

256] Actuates the piston

A] Piston

B] Push Rod
C] Primary cup
D] Check valve
257] Develops pressure on fluid
A] Piston
B] Push Rod
C] Primary cup
D] Check valve
258] Develops pressure on fuel to go out
A] Valves
B] Coil spring
C] Diaphragm
D] Rocker arm
259] Actuates the diaphragm
A] Valves
B] Coil spring
C] Diaphragm
D] Rocker arm
260] Person acts as a steerman of the vehicle is called
A] conductor
B] Driver
C] Passenger
D] spectator.
261] Act for leaving the vehicle in dangerous position
A] 125 of MV ACT 1988
B] 126 of MV ACT 1988
C] 128 of MV ACT 1988
D] 122 of MV ACT 1988
262] Act for Riding on running board
B] 126 of MV ACT 1988
C] 128 of MV ACT 1988
D] 122 of MV ACT 1988
E] 123 of MV ACT 1988
263] Act for Obstruction of driver
A] 125 of MV ACT 1988
B] 126 of MV ACT 1988
C] 128 of MV ACT 1988
D] 122 of MV ACT 1988

264] Act for Stationary vehicles
A] 125 of MV ACT 1988
B] <u>126 of MV ACT 1988</u>
C] 128 of MV ACT 1988
D] 122 of MV ACT 1988
265] Act for Safety measures for drivers and pillion riders
A] 125 of MV ACT 1988
B] 126 of MV ACT 1988
C] <u>128 of MV ACT 1988</u>
D] 122 of MV ACT 1988
266] Used to lift the vehicle
A] Pressure gauge
B] Oil tank
C] Oil spray gun
D] <u>Car hoist</u>
267] Used in car hoist
A] Pressure gauge
B] <u>Oil tank</u>
C] Oil spray gun
D] Car hoist
268] In diesel cycle Combustion takes place at
A] <u>Constant pressure</u>
B] Constant volume' '
C] Constant temperature
D] Constant temperature and pressure.
269] Rudolf Diesel, developed **a** Cl.engine
A] 1876
B] 1880
C] <u>1892</u>
D] 1930

Engine in vehicle

270] Perkins built 'P' series engines
A] 1876
B] 1880
C] 1892
D] <u>1930</u>
271] N.A OTTO developed a 4 stroke cycle engine
A] <u>1876</u>

B] 1880
C] 1892
D] 1930
272] Dugald Clerk developed a 2 stroke cycle engine
A] 1876
B] 1880
C] 1892
D] 1930
273] All cylinders in a horizontal line
A] 'V' Engine
B] Inline Engine
C] Opposed Engine
D] Radial Engine
274] Cylinders positioned in 'V' shape
A] 'V' Engine
B] Inline Engine
C] Opposed Engine
D] Radial Engine
275] Cylinders positioned radially
A] 'V' Engine
B] Inline Engine
C] Opposed Engine
D] Radial Engine
276] Cylinders arranged horizontally opposite to each other
A] 'V' Engine
B] Inline Engine
C] Opposed Engine
D] Radial Engine
277] Used as parking light Cum indicator
A] A symmetrical bulb
B] Miniature bulb
C] Festoon bulb
D] **S.C./ S.F.**
278] Used as no plate lampand brake lamp
B] Miniature bulb
C] Festoon bulb
D] **S.C / S.F.**
E] **D.C/ D.F.**

279] Used as two wheeler tail lamp
A] A symmetrical bulb
B] Miniature bulb
C] Festoon bulb
D] **S.C/ S.F.**
280] Used as panel instrument lamp
A] A symmetrical bulb
B] Miniature bulb
C] Festoon bulb
D] **S.C.IS.F.**
281] Used as headlight bulb
A] A symmetrical bulb
B] Miniature bulb
C] Festoon bulb
D] **S.C.IS.F.**
282] The head light parts can be replaced in
A] sealed beam
B] flush fitting type
C] prefocused bulb
D] halogen bulbs.
283] The head light is also used as
A] Side indicator
B] Stop indicator
C] Signalling device
D] Heating device.
284] To direct the shell light rays onto the road
A] Headlamp
B] Reflector
C] Lens
D] Adopter
285] To hold the bulb in the holder
A] Headlamp
B] Reflector
C] Lens
D] Adopter
286] To produce illumination
B] Reflector
C] Lens

D] Adopter

E] Bulb

287] To produce flat oval shaped beam

A] Headlamp

B] Reflector

C] Lens

D] Adopter

288] To hold the reflector in position

A] Headlamp

B] Reflector

C] Lens

D] Adopter

289] To indicate the vehicle is being braked

A] Headlight

B] Parking light

C] Stop light

D] Panel light

290] To read the working of gauges

A] Headlight

B] Parking light

C] Stop light

D] Panel light

291] To provide illumination on the road

A] Headlight

B] Parking light

C] Stop light

D] Panel light

292] to indicate the parking ' of vehicle

A] Headlight

B] Parking light

C] Stop light

D] Panel light

293] What IS the reason for hissing noise from cylinder head?

A] excessive tappet clearance

B] wrong injection timing

C] pie-ignition

D] air cleaner mounting loose.

294] Mounted on cylinder head or block

A] Fins
B] Radiators
C] Fan
D] Water pump
295] Allows fluid both way in and out of cylinder
A] Piston
B] Push Rod
C] Primary cup
D] Check valve
296] Relieves excess pressure of air from the air tank.
A] Air compressor
B] Unloader valve
C] Safety valve
D] Brake chamber

Air tank safety valve

297] Regulates maximum air pressure, reaching to air tank.
A] Air compressor
B] Unloader valve
C] Safety valve
D] Brake chamber
298] Supplies air to front and rear brake
A] Brake actuator
B] Dual brake valve
C] System protection valve
D] Flick valve

Brakes in car

299] Operated for parking the vehicle.
A] Brake actuator
B] Dual brake valve
C] System protection valve
D] Flick valve
300] Distributes air to various circuits
A] Brake actuator
B] Dual brake valve
C] System protection valve
301] Keeps valves in closed position
A] Push Rod
B] Tappet

C] Spring

D] Cam lobe

Engine valves

302] Allow fuel to flow in and out

A] Valves

B] Coil spring

C] Diaphragm

D] Rocker arm

Cooling system in car

303] Allows coolants into the expansion tank

A] Pressure relief valve

B] Engine fan belt

C] Radiator drain plug

D] Over flow pipe

304] An overflow valve is used

A] to send back excess fuel from the fuel filler

B] to supply more fuel to the fuel filter

C] to supply clean fuel

D]to take the leaking fuel

305] Feed pumps are driven by

A] camshaft of engine

B] Camshaft of FIP

C] Timing Gears

D] Varies from engine to engine.

306] The oil pumps are generally driven by

A] camshaft

B] rocker shaft

C] crankshaft

D] damper pulley

307]Engine develops less power due to

A]defective ignition timing

B]excessive rich mixture

C]defective lubrication system

D]too tight cylinder head

308] Creates pressure on fluid

A] Brake pedal

B] Master cylinder piston

C] Wheel cylinder piston

D] Distribution block

309] Pushes master cylinder piston through linkages.

A] Brake pedal

B] Master cylinder piston

C] Wheel cylinder piston

D] Distribution block

310] Actuates the piston

A] Piston

B] Push Rod

C] Primary cup

D] Check valve

311] Develops pressure on fluid

A] Piston

B] Push Rod

C] Primary cup

D] Check valve

Piston & rings in Engine

312] Displacement volume of piston

A] |.H.P.

B] Swept volume

C] Mechanical efficiency

D] Horse power

313] Starting point of piston's downward movement in the cylinder

A] T.D.C.

B] Cycle

C] B.D.C.

D] Ignition

314] Starting point of piston's upward movement in the cylinder

A] T.D.C.

B] Cycle

C] B.D.C.

D] Ignition

315] Prevents blow by

A] Piston

B] Piston pin

C] Connecting rod

D] Piston rings

316] Reciprocates in the cylinder

A] Piston
B] Piston pin
C] Connecting rod
D] Piston rings
317] Connects piston and connecting rod
A] Piston
B] Piston pin
C] Connecting rod
D] Piston rings
318] Oscillates in cylinder
A] Piston
B] Piston pin
C] Connecting rod
D] Piston rings
319]The top and bottom halves of connecting rod are bolted on
A] crankshaft man journal
B] crankpin journal
C] camshaft
D] piston pin boss
320] A hole is drilled between crankshaft main journal and crank pin for
A] balancing of crankshaft
B] reducing crankshaft weight
C] lubricating connecting rod bearings
D] reducing crankshaft vibrations
321] Converts reciprocating motion into rotary motion
A] Crankshaft
B] Flywheels
C] Torque wrench
D] Thrust bearing
322] Rotary movement to pull and push action
A] Wiper motor
B] Cranking link
C] **Pinion**
D] Wiper blade
323] Accommodates wheel hub bearings.
A] Kingpin
B] Spring pad
C] Stub axle shaft portion

D] Track rod ball joints
324] Pushes with drawal plate
A] Clutch cover
B] Release bearing
C] Release fingers
D] Clutch plate
325] **Takes thrust load**
A] Crankshaft
B] Flywheels
C] Torque wrench
D] Thrust bearing
326]Distributor shaft is supported by
A] ball bearing
B] shell bearing
C] bush bearing
D] needle bearing
327] Stores energy
A] Crankshaft
B] Flywheels
C] Torque wrench
D] Thrust bearing
328] engages with the flywheel ring
A] Pinion
B] Over running clutch
C] Plunger disk
D] Clutch
329] Flywheel magneto consists of
A] Temporary magnet
B] Bar magnet
C] Permanent magnet
D] Needle magnet.
330] in flywheel magneto, the ignition coil is
A] stationary
B] Moving
C] Rotating
D] Oscillating.
331] To rotate the permanent magnet
A] Switch

B] Secondary coils

C]Flywheels

D] Condensers

332] While reversing the vehicle the driver should control

A] Clutch

B] Forward gear

C] Accelerator

D] Hand brake.

333] The clutch plate assembly has a centre steel disc riveted with springs for

A] strength

B] flexibility

C] less noise

D] absorbing shocks

334] Dog clutches are used in

A] gear boxes

B] friction clutches

C] brakes

D] differentials

Dog clutches in vehicle

335] Synchromesh mechanisms is provided for

A] Increasing the speed of the vehicle

B] Reducing the speed of the vehicle

C] Smooth gear engagement'

D] None of the above.

336] Only spur gears are used

A] Sliding mesh

B] Synchromesh

C] Double declutching

D] Transfer case

337] Used for smooth gear shifting

A] Sliding mesh

B] Synchromesh

C] Double declutching

D] Transfer case

338] Hard gear shifting is due to

A] Worn out clutch disc

B] Damaged main shaft bearings

C] Synchronizer unit damaged

D] Excessive oil in the gearbox.

339] Gear slip is due to

A] Worn out synchroniser

B] Worn out clutch disc

C] Dry main shaft bearing

D] Weak pressure spring of clutch.

340] Noise in particular gear is due to

A] Insufficient clutch pedal free play

B] Damage gear teeth

C] Cracked gear box case

D] Damaged synchromesh unit.

341] Gearshift lever is used for

A] Releasing clutch

B] Changing gear

C] Increasing the speed of the engine

D] Controlling the direction of vehicle.

Steering gearbox in vehicle

342] In which type of steering gear box variable steering ration is achieved?

A] worm and roller steering gear

B] worm and nut steering gear

C] worm and sector steering gear

D] rack and pinion steering gear

Speed gear box in vehicle

343] The vehicle attains different speed by means of

A] gear box

B] clutch

C] differential

D] rear axle & wheel

344] Dog clutches are used in

A] gear boxes

B] friction clutches

C] brakes

D] differentials

345] in a 3 speed gear box in following combination of gears are provided

A] 3 forward and 1 reverse

B] 2 forward and 1 reverse

C] 4 forward

D] 2 forward and 2 reverse

346] which gear does not produce axial trust

A] spur gear

B] helical gear

C] spiral bevel gear

D] bevel gear

347] which gears converts rotary motion into linear motion

A] worm gears

B] herring bone gear

C] rack & pinion

D] helical gear

348] What is a reason for gear slip

A] unlubricated gear linka-ges

B] less oil in gear box

C] broken teeth of gear

D] wrong adjustment of gear lever

349] In a differential gear ratio can be calculated from any one of the following statements

A] sun gear

B] planetary gear

C] crown wheel

D] Pinion

Differential gear box in truck

350]The boiling temperature of the coolant in the cooling in the cooling system is increased by the use of

A]water jackets

B]vacuum valve only

C]pressure type radiator cap

D] radiator core tubes/pipes

Radiator cap in vehicle

351] The main purpose of pressure radiator cap is to

A]pressurize the system

B]increase air water circulation

C]help to develop vacuum in the system

D]avoid build up to pressure

352] one of the following causes may also contribute to overheating of an engine

A]clogged radiator cores

B]low idle speed setting

C]excessive valve tappet clearance

D]lubricating oil pressure is too high

353] Mounted on cylinder head or block

A] Fins

B] Radiators

C] Fan

D] Water pump

354] Drives the water pump

A] Pressure relief valve

B] Engine fan belt

C] Radiator drain plug

D] Over flow pipe

355] If thermostat valve remains in an open position then which of the following will happen

A]slow warming up to engine

B]engine will over heat

C]engine fails to start

D]stalling of engine

Thermostat valve in vehicle

356]In a dry sump lubrication system, a scavenging pump is used to

A] pump oil from sump to tank

B] pump oil directly to all moving parts

C] develop additional oil pressure

D] pump oil from tank to sum

357]Excessive oil pressure in the lubrication system may be due to

A] less quantity of engine oil in sump

B] incorrect adjustment of relief valve

C] less suction effect on the suction pipe

D] none of the above

358] Which component among the following reduces noise of exhaust gases?

A] Exhaust pipe

B] Muffler

C] inlet manifold

D] tail pipe.
359] Air compressor's driven by
A] To start heavy duty engine
B] Starter motor
C] Hydraulic cranking
D] <u>Electric motor</u>
360] Provides compressed air to system
A] <u>Air compressor</u>
B] Unloader valve
C] Safety valve
D] Brake chamber
361] Air compressors is used for
A] <u>Multipurpose</u>
B] To lift the car only
C] To lift and remove the wheel
D] To grind the chisel.
362] in the air compressor, the safety device is used to
A] To suck the air
B] To release the air completely
C] To regulate the air pressure
D] <u>To release excess air pressure</u>.
363] Used in air compressor
A] <u>Pressure gauge</u>
B] Oil tank
C] Oil spray gun
D] Car hoist
364] Cleans the air entering the cylinder
A] Air horn
B] Fuel bowl
C] <u>Air cleaner</u>
D] Air bleed
365] Carries fuel
A] Carburettor
B] Pump
C] Pipe lines
D] <u>Petrol tank</u>
366] Stores petrol
A] Carburettor

B] Pump
C] Pipe lines
D] Petrol tank
367] Delivers petrol to the engine
A] Carburettor
B] Pump
C] Pipe lines
D] Petrol tank

Fuel pump in Vehicle

368] Delivers petrol to carburettor
A] Carburettor
B] Pump
C] Pipe lines
D] Petrol tank
369] Holds petrol
A] Air horn
B] Fuel bowl
C] Air cleaner
D] Air bleed
370] if petrol air mixture is compressed in a cylinder
A] its volume reduces
B] its pressure will rise
C] its temperature will increase
D] all the above will happen
371]During suction stroke the charge drawn in a petrol engine is
A] air only
B. air and petrol mixture
C] petrol only
D] fuels other than petrol

Petrol engine in car

372] In a petrol engine air fuel mixture is drawn into the cylinder due to vacuum created during
A] power stroke
B] exhaust stroke
C] suction stroke
D] compression stroke
373] the high fuel consumption of a petrol engine may be due to
A] leakage of fuel from carburetor

B] defects in lubrication system
C] air leaks in intake manifold
D] incorrect idle speed (too low]
374] the float circuit is provided in a carburetor
A] to store fuel vapours
B] to supply mixture of air & fuel
C] to maintain proper level of fuel in float chamber
D] none of the above
375] increase or decrease the speed of the engine
B] Speedometer
C] Clutch pedal
D] Ignition switch
E] Accelerator
376] While allowing other vehicle to overtake
A] Accelerate
B] Reduce accelerator
C] Stop the vehicle
D] Move the vehicle to right.
377] Fuel catching fire
A] T.D.C.
B] Cycle
C] B.D.C.
D] Ignition
378] To seal the tank externally.
A] Baffles
B] Filter cap
C] Passage in the baffle
D] Filler neck
379] Prevents slashing of fuel in the tank
A] Baffles
B] Filter cap
C] Passage in the baffle
D] Filler neck
380] To fill fuel in the tank
A] Baffles
B] Filter cap
C] Passage in the baffle
D] Filler neck

381] To transfer fuel from one compartment to other compartment
A] Baffles
B] Filter cap
C] Passage in the baffle
D] Filler neck
382] Moving coil instrument works on the effect of...
A] chemical effect
B] heating effect
C] electrostatic effect
D] electromagnetic effect
383] Battery power
A] To start heavy duty engine
B] Starter motor
C] Hydraulic cranking
D] Electric motor

Starter winding armature in vehicle

384] connect two terminals of solenoid.
A] Pinion
B] Over running clutch
C] Plunger disk
D] Clutch
385] When the horn button is pressed the current flows to horn through
A] Horn switch
B] Solenoid coil
C] Battery
D] Chassis.
386] Turns core to magnet
A] Solenoid Switch
B] Actuating wire (when heated]
C] Ballast Resistors
D] Actuating wire (when cooled]
387] The alternator in a car delivers 4A and has a load of 3 ohms connected across its terminals. Find the voltage of the circuit
A] 18V
B] 24V
C] 12V
D] 16V

Dynamo (Alternator) distributor cap in Engine

INDUSTRIAL TRAINING INSTITUTE

Monthly Test-1, Marks- 20, Date:- _______________

(Every Question Carry Two Marks)

1-06] Benefit of SS system is ------

A] Increase in productivity

B] Increase in quality

C] Reduction in wastage of time

D] All of these

2-07] Safety is -----------

A] Nobody's business

B] Every bodise business

C] Some bodies business

D] The organization business

3-08] For basic categories of safety signs are available The meaning of "prohibition" sign ----

A] Shows it must not be done

B] Shows what must be done

C] Warns the hazard or danger

D] Gives information of safety provision

4-09] Which one is a workshop safety?

A] Keep shop floor clean and free from grease, oil or other slippery materials

B] Stop the machine before changing the speed

C] Don't use cracked or chipped tools

D] Don't try to stop a running machine with hand

5-10] In Personal Protect Equipment (PPE] HELMET is used to

A] Protect head

B] Protect eyes

C] Protect hands

D] Protect ears

6-11] Which of the following belongs to general safety?

A Have a worker in good attitude

B] The work clean and clear

C] Concentrate on your work

D] Keep the floor and gangways clean and clear

7-12] While grinding, which is used to protect the eyes?

A] Dark green glass

B] Mask

C] Sun glasses

D] Safety goggles

8-13] Which of the following is done for machine safety?

A] Check the oil level before starting the machine

B] Do things in a methodical way

C] Keep the floor and gangways clean and clear

D] Don't use dies and scarves

9-14] ln Personal Protect Equipment (PPE], 'sleeves' is used to protect ----------

A] Face

B] Eyes

C] Ears

D] Hands

10-15] ABC stands for -------------

A] Automatic Breathing Control

B] Automatic Blood Control

C] Airway Breathing Circulation

D] Automatic Blood Circulation

INDUSTRIAL TRAINING INSTITUTE

Monthly Test-2, Marks- 20, Date:- ______________

(Every Question Carry Two Marks)

1-21] The instrument used to mark parallel lines, parallel to the datum edge is -

A] Jenny caliper

B] Divider

C] Outside calliper

D] Inside calliper

2-22] Which one of the following is an indirect measuring tool?

A] Outside caliper

B] Vernier calliper

C] Steel rule

D] Outside micrometer

3-23] The reference surface during marking is provided by the...

A] Surface gauge

B] Workpiece

C] Drawing of the work

D] Marking table surface

4-24] The part of the universal surface gauge which helps to draw a parallel line along a datum edge is the..

A] Rocker arm

B] Snug

C] Fine adjustment screw

D] Guide pins

5-25] Scribers are made of...

A] Mild steel

B] High carbon steel

C] Brass

D] Cast iron

6-26] Portion of the hammer used for fixing the handle is...

A] Face

B] Peen

C] Cheek

D] Eye hole

7-27] Weight of the hammer for the marking purpose is...

A] 250g

B] 500g

C] 1 kg

D] 2 kgs

8-28] The size of the dividers are specified by the...

A] Total length of the legs

B] Distance between the points when fully opened

C] Length of legs without the points

D] Distance between the pivot and the point

9-29] Name the punch used to locate the centre.

A] Prick punch 30°

B] Prick punch 60°

C] Centre punch

D] Dot punch

10-30] The point angle of centre punch is --------

A] 30°

B] 50°

c] 900

D] 1200

INDUSTRIAL TRAINING INSTITUTE

Monthly Test-3, Marks- 20, Date:- ______________

(Every Question Carry Two Marks)

1-36] The size of an engineer's vice is specified by the...

A] Length of the movable jaw

B] Width of the jaws

C] Height of the vice

D] Maximum opening of the jaws

2-37] The point angle of scriber is -----------

A] 30°

B] 60°

C] 5° to 10°

D] 12° to 15°

3-38] The cutting angle for chipping cast iron is...

A] 37.5?

B] 55?

C] 60?

D] 90?

4-39] The chisel will dig into the material when...

A] The rake angle is more

B] The clearance angle is too low

C] The angle of inclination is more

D] The angle of inclination is too low

5-40] A slight convexity is given to the cutting edge to...

A] Cut curved surfaces

B] Cut sharp corners

C] Prevent digging of the ends

D] Allow the lubricant to enter

6-41] Surface plates are made of...

A] High grade cast steel

B] Fine-grained cast iron

C] Alloy steels

D] Wrought iron

7-42] Surface plates are specified by their length and breadth & are in

A] decimetre

B] Cubic meter

C] Cylindrical

8-43] Used on finished tubular wrench surfaces to avoid marking.

A] Stillson pipe

B] Chain wrench

C] Strap wrench

D] Footprint wrench

9-44] Used for gripping and turning pipes and round stocks in confined places.

A] Stillson pipe

B] Chain wrench

C] Strap wrench

D] Footprint wrench

10-45] Used for holding iarge diameter pipes.

A] Stillson pipe

B] Chain wrench

C] Strap wrench

D] Footprint wrench

INDUSTRIAL TRAINING INSTITUTE

Monthly Test-4, Marks- 20, Date:- ______________

(Every Question Carry Two Marks)

1-266] Used to lift the vehicle

A] Pressure gauge

B] Oil tank

C] Oil spray gun

D] Car hoist

2-267] Used in car hoist

A] Pressure gauge

B] Oil tank

C] Oil spray gun

D] Car hoist

3-268] In diesel cycle Combustion takes place at

A] Constant pressure

B] Constant volume' '

C] Constant temperature

D] Constant temperature and pressure.

4-269] Rudolf Diesel, developed a Cl.engine

A] 1876

B] 1880

C] 1892

D] 1930

5-270] Perkins built 'P' series engines

A] 1876

B] 1880
C] 1892
D] 1930
6-271] N.A OTTO developed a 4 stroke cycle engine
A] 1876
B] 1880
C] 1892
D] 1930
7-272] Dugald Clerk developed a 2 stroke cycle engine
A] 1876
B] 1880
C] 1892
D] 1930
8-273] All cylinders in a horizontal line
A] 'V' Engine
B] Inline Engine
C] Opposed Engine
D] Radial Engine
9-274] Cylinders positioned in 'V' shape
A] 'V' Engine
B] Inline Engine
C] Opposed Engine
D] Radial Engine
10-275] Cylinders positioned radially
A] 'V' Engine
B] Inline Engine
C] Opposed Engine
D] Radial Engine

INDUSTRIAL TRAINING INSTITUTE

Monthly Test-5, Marks- 20, Date:- ______________

(Every Question Carry Two Marks)

1-276] Cylinders arranged horizontally opposite to each other
A] 'V' Engine
B] Inline Engine
C] Opposed Engine
D] Radial Engine
2-277] Used as parking light Cum indicator
A] A symmetrical bulb

B] Miniature bulb
C] Festoon bulb
D] S.C./ S.F.
3-278] Used as no plate lamp and brake lamp
B] Miniature bulb
C] Festoon bulb
D] S.C / S.F.
E] D.C/ D.F.
4-279] Used as two wheeler tail lamp
A] A symmetrical bulb
B] Miniature bulb
C] Festoon bulb
D] S.C/ S.F.
5-280] Used as panel instrument lamp
A] A symmetrical bulb
B] Miniature bulb
C] Festoon bulb
D] S.C.IS.F.
6-281] Used as headlight bulb
A] A symmetrical bulb
B] Miniature bulb
C] Festoon bulb
D] S.C.IS.F.
7-282] The head light parts can be replaced in
A] sealed beam
B] flush fitting type
C] prefocused bulb
D] halogen bulbs.
8-283] The head light is also used as
A] Side indicator
B] Stop indicator
C] Signalling device
D] Heating device.
9-284] To direct the shell light rays onto the road
A] Headlamp
B] Reflector
C] Lens
D] Adopter

10-285] To hold the bulb in the holder
A] Headlamp
B] Reflector
C] Lens
D] Adopter

INDUSTRIAL TRAINING INSTITUTE

Monthly Test-6, Marks- 20, Date:- ______________

(Every Question Carry Two Marks)

1-286] To produce illumination
B] Reflector
C] Lens
D] Adopter
E] Bulb

2-287] To produce flat oval shaped beam
A] Headlamp
B] Reflector
C] Lens
D] Adopter

3-288] To hold the reflector in position
A] Headlamp
B] Reflector
C] Lens
D] Adopter

4-289] To indicate the vehicle is being braked
A] Headlight
B] Parking light
C] Stop light
D] Panel light

5-290] To read the working of gauges
A] Headlight
B] Parking light
C] Stop light
D] Panel light

6-291] To provide illumination on the road
A] Headlight
B] Parking light
C] Stop light
D] Panel light

7-292] to indicate the parking ' of vehicle
A] Headlight
B] Parking light
C] Stop light
D] Panel light
8-293] What IS the reason for hissing noise from cylinder head?
A] excessive tappet clearance
B] wrong injection timing
C] pie-ignition
D] air cleaner mounting loose.
9-294] Mounted on cylinder head or block
A] Fins
B] Radiators
C] Fan
D] Water pump
10-295] Allows fluid both way in and out of cylinder
A] Piston
B] Push Rod
C] Primary cup
D] Check valve

INDUSTRIAL TRAINING INSTITUTE

Monthly Test-7, Marks- 20, Date:- ______________

(Every Question Carry Two Marks)

1-296] Relieves excess pressure of air from the air tank.
A] Air compressor
B] Unloader valve
C] Safety valve
D] Brake chamber
2-297] Regulates maximum air pressure, reaching to air tank.
A] Air compressor
B] Unloader valve
C] Safety valve
D] Brake chamber
3-298] Supplies air to front and rear brake
A] Brake actuator
B] Dual brake valve
C] System protection valve
D] Flick valve

4-299] Operated for parking the vehicle.
A] Brake actuator
B] Dual brake valve
C] System protection valve
D] Flick valve
5-300] Distributes air to various circuits
A] Brake actuator
B] Dual brake valve
C] System protection valve
6-301] Keeps valves in closed position
A] Push Rod
B] Tappet
C] Spring
D] Cam lobe
7-302] Allow fuel to flow in and out
A] Valves
B] Coil spring
C] Diaphragm
D] Rocker arm
8-303] Allows coolants into the expansion tank
A] Pressure relief valve
B] Engine fan belt
C] Radiator drain plug
D] Over flow pipe
9-304] An overflow valve is used
A] to send back excess fuel from the fuel filler
B] to supply more fuel to the fuel filter
C] to supply clean fuel
D] to take the leaking fuel
10-305] Feed pumps are driven by
A] camshaft of engine
B] Camshaft of FIP
C] Timing Gears
D] Varies from engine to engine.

INDUSTRIAL TRAINING INSTITUTE

Monthly Test-8, Marks- 20, Date:- _______________

(Every Question Carry Two Marks)

1-306] The oil pumps are generally driven by

A] camshaft
B] rocker shaft
C] crankshaft
D] damper pulley
2-307]Engine develops less power due to
A]defective ignition timing
B]excessive rich mixture
C]defective lubrication system
D]too tight cylinder head
3-308] Creates pressure on fluid
A] Brake pedal
B] Master cylinder piston
C] Wheel cylinder piston
D] Distribution block
4-309] Pushes master cylinder piston through linkages.
A] Brake pedal
B] Master cylinder piston
C] Wheel cylinder piston
D] Distribution block
5-310] Actuates the piston
A] Piston
B] Push Rod
C] Primary cup
D] Check valve
6-311] Develops pressure on fluid
A] Piston
B] Push Rod
C] Primary cup
D] Check valve
7-312] Displacement volume of piston
A] |.H.P.
B] Swept volume
C] Mechanical efficiency
D] Horse power
8-313] Starting point of piston's downward movement in the cylinder
A] T.D.C.
B] Cycle
C] B.D.C.

D] Ignition

9-314] Starting point of piston's upward movement in the cylinder

A] T.D.C.

B] Cycle

C] B.D.C.

D] Ignition

10-315] Prevents blow by

A] Piston

B] Piston pin

C] Connecting rod

D] Piston rings

INDUSTRIAL TRAINING INSTITUTE

Monthly Test-9, Marks- 20, Date:- ______________

(Every Question Carry Two Marks)

1-316] Reciprocates in the cylinder

A] Piston

B] Piston pin

C] Connecting rod

D] Piston rings

2-317] Connects piston and connecting rod

A] Piston

B] Piston pin

C] Connecting rod

D] Piston rings

3-318] Oscillates in cylinder

A] Piston

B] Piston pin

C] Connecting rod

D] Piston rings

4-319]The top and bottom halves of connecting rod are bolted on

A] crankshaft man journal

B] crankpin journal

C] camshaft

D] piston pin boss

5-320] A hole is drilled between crankshaft main journal and crank pin for

A] balancing of crankshaft

B] reducing crankshaft weight

C] lubricating connecting rod bearings

D] reducing crankshaft vibrations

6-321] Converts reciprocating motion into rotary motion

A] Crankshaft

B] Flywheels

C] Torque wrench

D] Thrust bearing

7-322] Rotary movement to pull and push action

A] Wiper motor

B] Cranking link

C] Pinion

D] Wiper blade

8-323] Accommodates wheel hub bearings.

A] Kingpin

B] Spring pad

C] Stub axle shaft portion

D] Track rod ball joints

9-324] Pushes with drawal plate

A] Clutch cover

B] Release bearing

C] Release fingers

D] Clutch plate

10-325] Takes thrust load

A] Crankshaft

B] Flywheels

C] Torque wrench

D] Thrust bearing

INDUSTRIAL TRAINING INSTITUTE

Monthly Test-10, Marks- 20, Date:- ______________

(Every Question Carry Two Marks)

1-326]Distributor shaft is supported by

A] ball bearing

B] shell bearing

C] bush bearing

D] needle bearing

2-327] Stores energy

A] Crankshaft

B] Flywheels

C] Torque wrench
D] Thrust bearing
3-328] engages with the flywheel ring
A] Pinion
B] Over running clutch
C] Plunger disk
D] Clutch
4-329] Flywheel magneto consists of
A] Temporary magnet
B] Bar magnet
C] Permanent magnet
D] Needle magnet.
5-330] in flywheel magneto, the ignition coil is
A] stationary
B] Moving
C] Rotating
D] Oscillating.
6-331] To rotate the permanent magnet
A] Switch
B] Secondary coils
C] Flywheels
D] Condensers
7-332] While reversing the vehicle the driver should control
A] Clutch
B] Forward gear
C] Accelerator
D] Hand brake.
8-333] The clutch plate assembly has a centre steel disc riveted with springs for
A] strength
B] flexibility
C] less noise
D] absorbing shocks
9-334] Dog clutches are used in
A] gear boxes
B] friction clutches
C] brakes
D] differentials

10-335] Synchromesh mechanisms is provided for
A] Increasing the speed of the vehicle
B] Reducing the speed of the vehicle
C] Smooth gear engagement'
D] None of the above.

INDUSTRIAL TRAINING INSTITUTE

Monthly Test-11, Marks- 20, Date:- ______________

(Every Question Carry Two Marks)

1-336] Only spur gears are used
A] Sliding mesh
B] Synchromesh
C] Double declutching
D] Transfer case
2-337] Used for smooth gear shifting
A] Sliding mesh
B] Synchromesh
C] Double declutching
D] Transfer case
3-338] Hard gear shifting is due to
A] Worn out clutch disc
B] Damaged main shaft bearings
C] Synchronizer unit damaged
D] Excessive oil in the gearbox.
4-339] Gear slip is due to
A] Worn out synchroniser
B] Worn out clutch disc
C] Dry main shaft bearing
D] Weak pressure spring of clutch.
5-340] Noise in particular gear is due to
A] Insufficient clutch pedal free play
B] Damage gear teeth
C] Cracked gear box case
D] Damaged synchromesh unit.
6-341] Gearshift lever is used for
A] Releasing clutch
B] Changing gear
C] Increasing the speed of the engine
D] Controlling the direction of vehicle.

7-342] In which type of steering gear box variable steering ration is achieved?

A] worm and roller steering gear

B] worm and nut steering gear

C] worm and sector steering gear

D] rack and pinion steering gear

8-343] The vehicle attains different speed by means of

A] gear box

B] clutch

C] differential

D] rear axle & wheel

9-344] Dog clutches are used in

A] gear boxes

B] friction clutches

C] brakes

D] differentials

10-345] in a 3 speed gear box in following combination of gears are provided

A] 3 forward and 1 reverse

B] 2 forward and 1 reverse

C] 4 forward

D] 2 forward and 2 reverse

INDUSTRIAL TRAINING INSTITUTE

Monthly Test-12, Marks- 20, Date:- ______________

(Every Question Carry Two Marks)

1-346] which gear does not produce axial trust

A] spur gear

B] helical gear

C] spiral bevel gear

D] bevel gear

2-347] which gears converts rotary motion into linear motion

A] worm gears

B] herring bone gear

C] rack & pinion

D] helical gear

3-348] What is a reason for gear slip

A] unlubricated gear linka-ges

B] less oil in gear box

C] broken teeth of gear

D] wrong adjustment of gear lever

4-349] In a differential gear ratio can be calculated from any one of the following statements

A] sun gear

B] planetary gear

C] crown wheel

D] Pinion

5-350]The boiling temperature of the coolant in the cooling in the cooling system is increased by the use of

A]water jackets

B]vacuum valve only

C]pressure type radiator cap

D] radiator core tubes/pipes

6-351] The main purpose of pressure radiator cap is to

A]pressurize the system

B]increase air water circulation

C]help to develop vacuum in the system

D]avoid build up to pressure

7-352] one of the following causes may also contribute to overheating of an engine

A]clogged radiator cores

B]low idle speed setting

C]excessive valve tappet clearance

D]lubricating oil pressure is too high

8-353] Mounted on cylinder head or block

A] Fins

B] Radiators

C] Fan

D] Water pump

9-354] Drives the water pump

A] Pressure relief valve

B] Engine fan belt

C] Radiator drain plug

D] Over flow pipe

10-355] If thermostat valve remains in an open position then which of the following will happen

A]slow warming up to engine

B]engine will over heat
C]engine fails to start
D]stalling of engine

www.ingramcontent.com/pod-product-compliance
Ingram Content Group UK Ltd.
Pitfield, Milton Keynes, MK11 3LW, UK
UKHW021923190726
13853UKWH00002B/806

9 798886 673753